Science on Trial

written by Jillian Powell
illustrated by Gary Andrews and Chris Brown

CONTENTS

Our changing world

Science is changing our world today, just as it has done for thousands of years.

FACT: In 1614, the scientist Galileo Galilei changed our view of the universe with his theory that the Earth orbited the Sun. The Catholic Church put him on trial for daring to suggest that the Earth was not the centre of God's universe.

Science can change the way we live our lives – think, for example, of the invention of electric lighting, television, the car or the aeroplane.

Medical discoveries have helped us live longer and healthier lives. **Antibiotics** and other drugs cure many diseases, and vaccination prevents others.

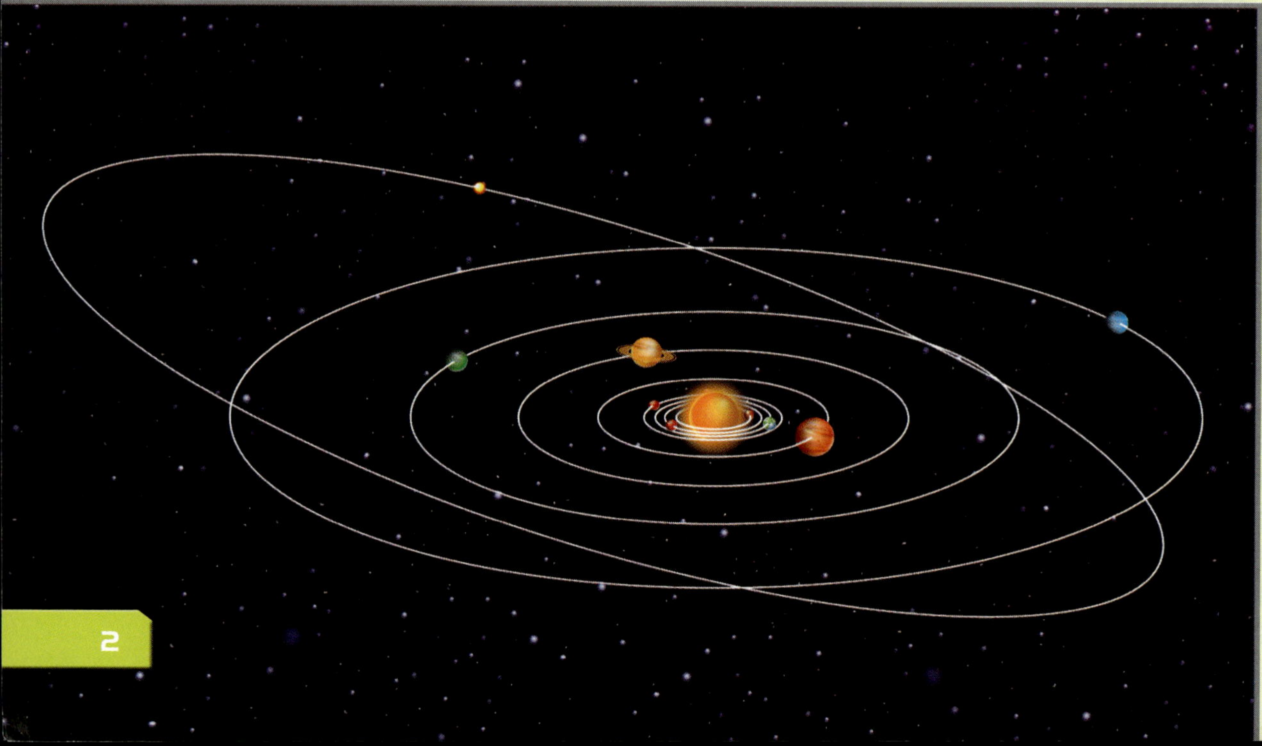

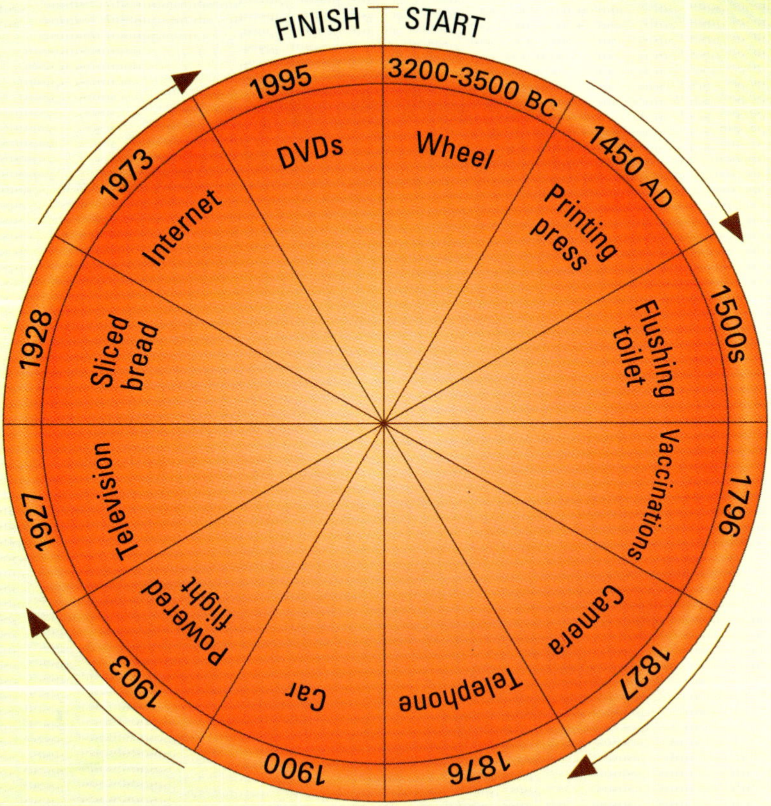

Science also changes the way we think about ourselves and our world. Today, the science of **genetics** is revealing how much we inherit in our **genes**, not just the way we look, but our health and abilities, and perhaps our personality and behaviour.

Scientific discoveries can be used to change the world in good or bad ways. The discovery of **radioactivity** by Marie Curie in 1898 led to many lives being saved by the use of X-rays. But radiation also became a deadly weapon in atomic bombs.

Discoveries in medicine, genetics, space science and electronics all raise important questions about how we want to change our world and how we want to live our lives. There are some practical problems, and some questions of right and wrong. **As science goes on trial, some will argue for, some against: we must all decide.**

Marie Curie's discovery of radiation led to the development of medical X-rays.

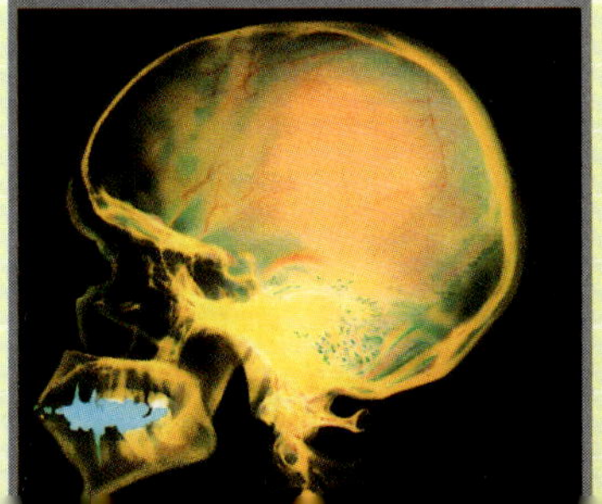

Radiation became a deadly weapon in atomic bombs.

Cars – the best or the worst invention of the twentieth century?

Science Box

Cars use **internal-combustion engines** which were invented in 1876. These engines burn **fossil fuels**. A spark ignites a mixture of air and fuel, which drives the engine. The process also releases a mixture of gases including carbon dioxide, one of the main **greenhouse gases** responsible for global warming.

FOR

Before cars, the only ways of getting around were by foot, bicycle, horses or trains. Travelling long distances was slow and uncomfortable. Cars made it possible for us to travel faster and more comfortably.

Cars give us freedom of movement. We can travel where we want, when we want. We use them to get to schools and workplaces, to go shopping and to visit family and friends. They are a comfortable and convenient way of getting around.

Many people like to do a big weekly shop at an out-of-town supermarket and carry their shopping home in the car. Business and science parks are often on the edge of towns so people need their cars to get to work. Children need to get to school and it may be too far to walk or cycle.

Cars mean that families can go out for day trips, or go on holiday and carry all their luggage with them.

Public transport is not as convenient as cars. It may not run when or where you want it to. People have to queue and wait, sometimes in the cold and rain. Buses and trains can be crowded and dirty. For people who are old or disabled, a car may be the best way of getting about.

We need cars for the way we live today.

AGAINST

Cars have changed people's lives over the past century. Now they are changing our planet. The number of cars on the roads is expected to reach 1000 million by 2025. This will mean more pollution, noise and traffic jams.

Cars are damaging the environment. Air pollution from cars mixes with moisture in rain clouds to form **acid rain** which kills trees and plants and damages buildings. In cities, air pollution can reach dangerous levels. Sunlight combines with polluted air to make a poisonous smog. The smog is especially harmful to children and people with breathing problems like asthma.

FACT: A car produces four times its own weight in carbon dioxide each year. Scientists are now designing cars powered by electricity and petrol, or "lean burn" cars, which use less fuel and reduce exhaust gases.

A forest killed by acid rain

Modern cars are fitted with exhaust cleaning systems but these can produce more nitrous oxide. Nitrous oxide and carbon dioxide are greenhouse gases. They trap heat from sunlight in the Earth's atmosphere, causing **global warming**. This is changing the Earth's **climate** and weather. There are more floods, **droughts** and storms. If the Earth warms enough for the polar icecaps to melt, sea levels will rise and huge areas of land will be flooded.

Cars burn millions of tonnes of fuel every year and use huge amounts of raw materials such as copper and steel. Destroying old and unwanted cars also damages the environment because many materials are difficult to recycle. Old cars pile up on scrap heaps and in landfill sites.

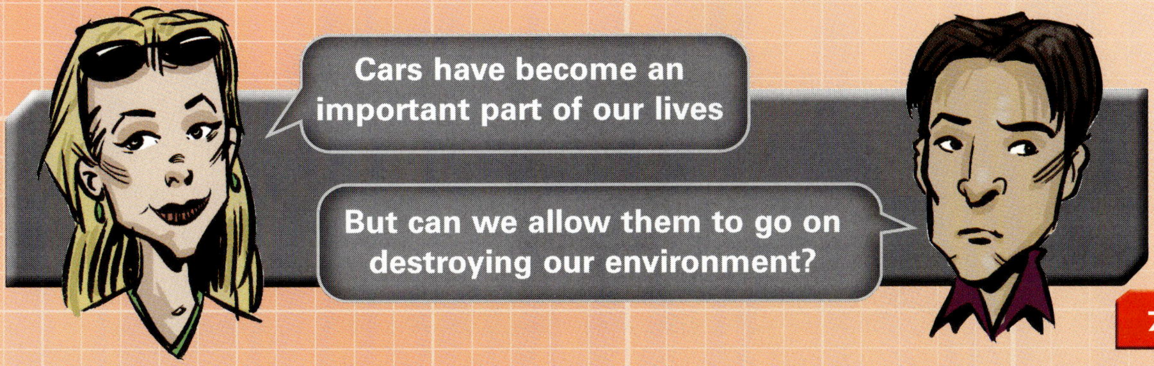

Animal testing - kill or cure?

Science Box

Scientists use laboratory animals to test new drugs, vaccines and consumer products to make sure they are safe for people to use. They also use animals in biomedical research, such as research into growing tissue from stem cells.

FOR

Animal testing played an important part in many major medical advances of the last century. Scientists have developed many modern drugs such as antibiotics, vaccines and **anaesthetics** by testing them on animals first.

Vaccines developed with animal testing save thousands of lives.

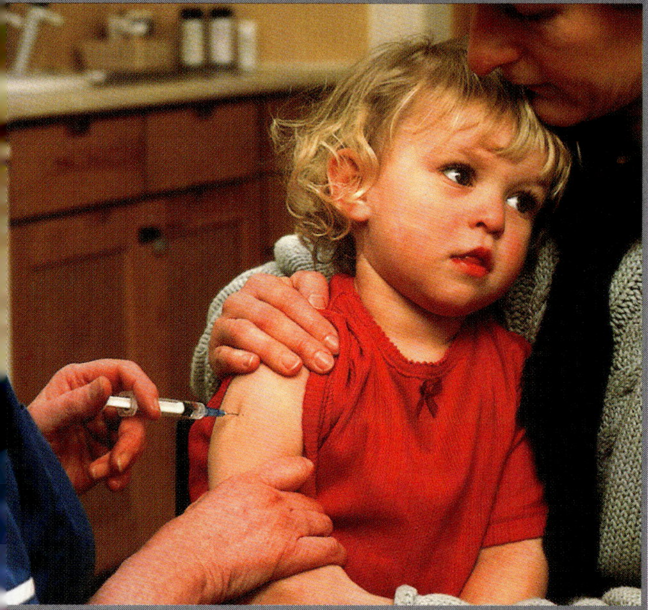

Many people who want to ban animal testing have benefited from medicines and drugs that were tested on animals. A ban on animal testing would slow down many areas of medical research as well as the development of better, safer drugs.

The scientists who work with animals in laboratories care about the animals and make sure that they are well fed and housed. They consult vets to make sure that animals suffer the minimum of pain or distress during tests. The testing often only consists of taking a blood sample, giving an injection or changing an animal's diet. In other cases painkillers are used to stop the animal feeling pain.

No other method of research could completely replace animal testing. Animals may help scientists find cures for diseases such as cancer, AIDS and heart disease.

Some drugs can relieve the symptoms of asthma, but animal testing may develop a complete cure.

AGAINST

Animals are living creatures that have rights just as people do. They have a right to live a normal life in their natural **habitat**. Scientists cannot know how animals feel, or what pain or distress they suffer during tests and experiments.

Penicillin is a drug that helps save thousands of lives. But it kills guinea pigs. If it had been tested on them, it might have been rejected for humans too.

People are different from animals and suffer from different illnesses and diseases. Animal testing is unreliable because drugs can have different effects on animals and people. A drug that is passed as safe after animal testing may have **side-effects** on the people who use it.

Alternatives to animal testing exist. Scientists can use **computer modelling**, or use human tissue in the laboratory for research. They can also study people and populations. New scanning techniques mean that they can use people to find out for example, about blood flow and nerve activity in the brain.

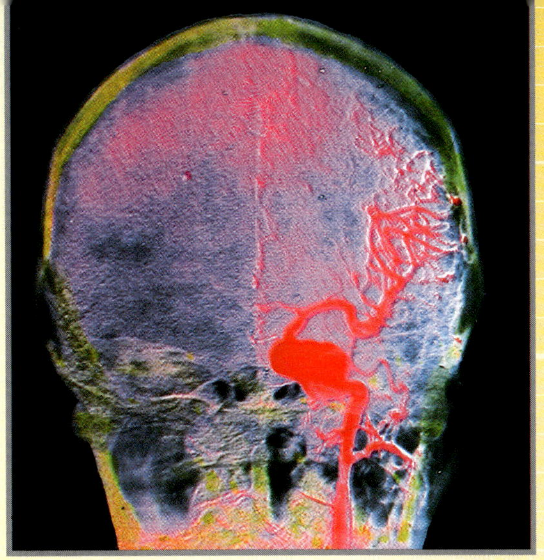

Many pointless and unnecessary tests are carried out on animals, for example for products like shampoos and make-up.

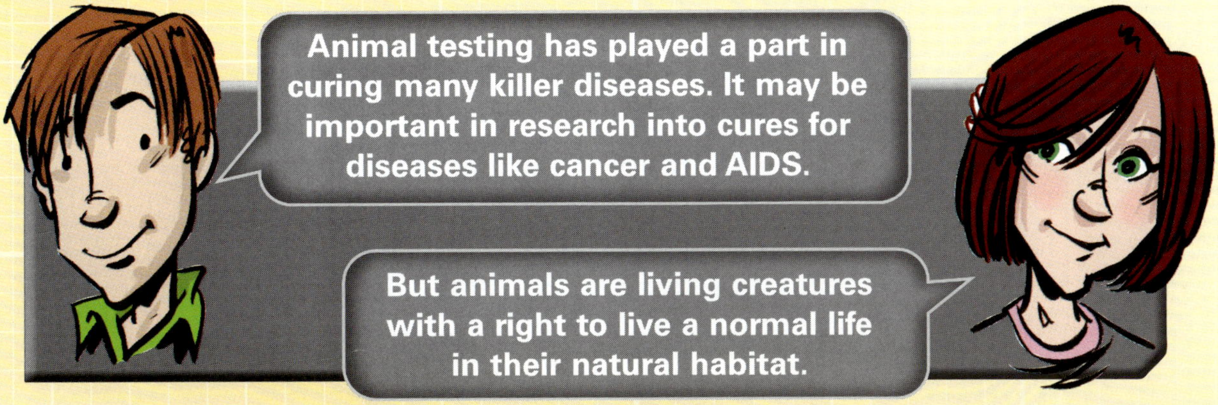

Genetic modification – improving on nature?

Science Box

Genetic modification means moving individual genes from one plant or animal to another. This can make them grow faster or fight off diseases better. Scientists do this by "gene splicing". This means breaking open the plant or animal's own genetic material, introducing new material from another species, then stitching it all together to form a new gene.

FOR

For hundreds of years, farmers and plant breeders have been changing the food we eat by selective breeding. They have learned to **cross-breed** the best plants and animals to produce stronger, faster-growing animals and better crops. Some people think that genetic modification is just a faster, better way of doing this.

Genetic modification can help us feed the world, especially in developing countries, which face hunger because of drought or war.

FACT: The world population is now over six billion, and is expected to reach about eight billion by 2025. Already 800 million people go hungry every year.

Scientists can put a gene in crops to protect them against pests and diseases. This means that farmers will not need to use so many harmful chemicals to protect their crops. Scientists can also add genes that help crops to survive drought or frosts or to grow on poor or salty soil. This will mean bigger, better crops can be grown even where the land or climate is poor.

FACT: The first genetically modified soy beans were harvested in 1996. The beans had been injected with a gene that made them resistant to the weed killer glyphosate. This meant the weeds in the soy fields could be sprayed with glyphosate – which normally kills all vegetation – and the soy beans would survive.

Scientists can design the foods that we want, like growing potatoes that are ideal for making crisps, or wheat that is ideal for bread-making. They can alter fresh foods like strawberries so they ripen more slowly and stay fresh longer. This means they can be kept longer in the supermarkets, and there will be less waste.

Genetic modification will help us grow and store the food we need, and feed the world's growing population in the future.

AGAINST

Genetic modification is disturbing the building blocks of nature. Scientists are mixing genes of species that would not breed together naturally. For example, they have put genes from a fish into tomatoes so that the tomatoes are resistant to frost.

There is a risk that genes which cause **allergies** will be passed from one food to another. Genes in plant or animal foods could make people resistant to antibiotics. This would mean that if we are ill, antibiotics will no longer cure us.

FACT: When soy beans were injected with genes from Brazil nuts, they caused allergic reactions in people with a nut allergy.

Genetically modified animals and plants might be so strong that they make other species die out. Pollen from genetically modified crops can be carried by the wind or insects and fertilise other crops. Genes that resist weed killers could be passed to weeds and create a breed of super-weeds.

If crops can resist strong pesticides, farmers may begin to use more pesticides, not fewer.

Genetically modified crops may not help farmers or their families in developing countries. They may be forced out of business by larger farms which can afford the new **bio-technology**. Only two per cent of genetically modified foods are changed in order to improve taste and **nutrition**. The rest are altered to make food production and processing faster for the big food companies.

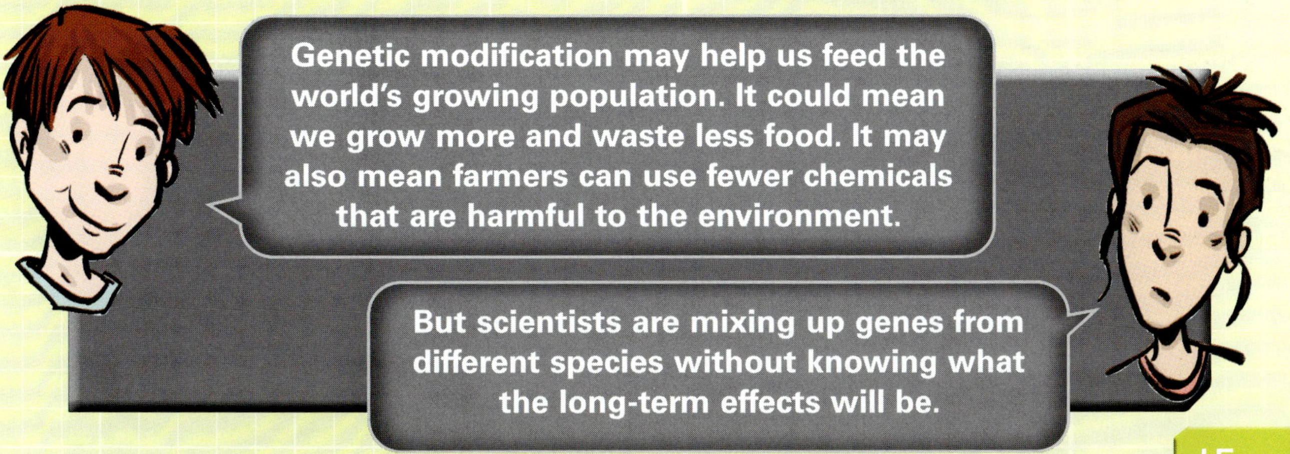

Cloning – changing what it means to be human?

Cloning means making an exact copy of an **organism** or a cell.

Science Box

Reproductive cloning means making an identical copy of a whole human being or animal. *Therapeutic cloning* means growing individual parts of the body to be used in operations on patients who might need, for example, a new liver or some new skin.

FOR

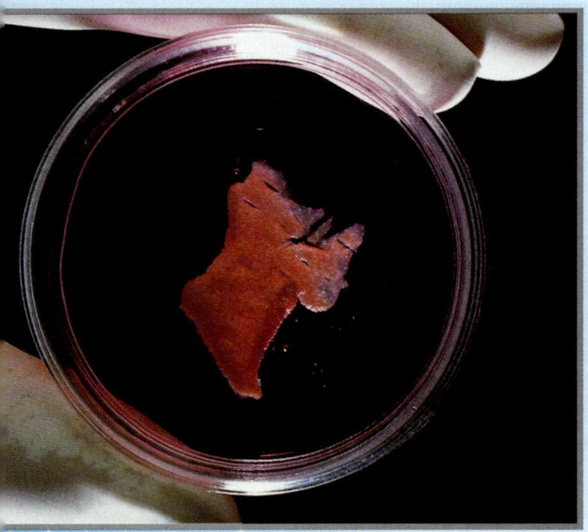

Therapeutic cloning, that is cloning used for **therapy**, may help us cure many diseases. Learning how to replace unhealthy or damaged cells may even help scientists cure cancer.

Scientists could use therapeutic cloning to repair or replace damaged tissue or organs in the human body. They would do this by taking **stem cells** from human **embryos**. Stem cells are special types of cell which can be reprogrammed to become any other type of body cell.

Scientists can use stem cells to make new skin for burn victims, or to grow replacement organs such as heart, liver and lungs. For example, they may be able to reverse the damage caused by heart attacks by cloning healthy heart cells and injecting them into the affected area of the heart. Cloned organs and tissue would not be rejected by the body's **immune system** as some **transplanted** organs are now.

Reproductive cloning would create an identical copy of a person, like identical twins.

Scientists could use reproductive cloning to make babies for couples who cannot have children naturally. They could even make clones of children who have died. Clones could mean that we can make copies of ourselves to live in the future. Scientists may also learn how to reverse the ageing process from the science of cloning, so we can all stay young and live longer.

AGAINST

Cloning allows scientists to interfere with nature by creating animals and humans in a laboratory. Every human being is unique. We each inherit our genes from our two parents. But cloning means that a person can be created from just one parent. It also means we might no longer have natural family relationships, because one person could produce many clones that were identical to him or her.

Human clones could be created to provide replacements for dead people, or to act as organ donors to provide spare parts. This might undermine our dignity and individuality as human beings.

The idea of cloning has inspired novels and television dramas such as *The Cloning of Joanna May*.

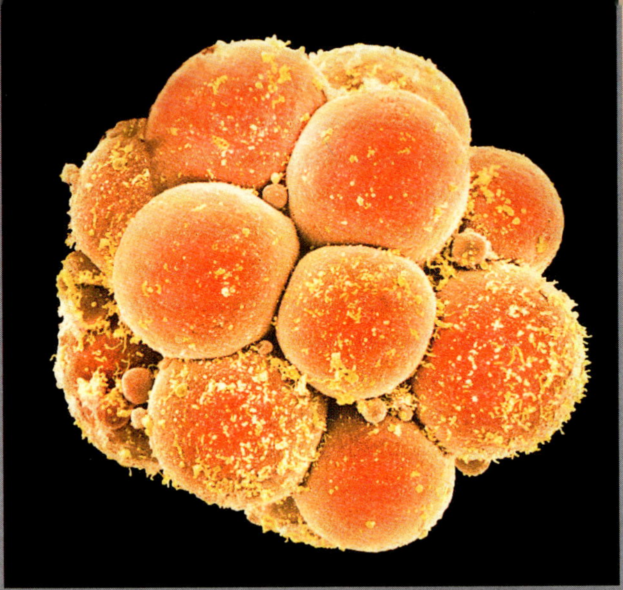

If stem cells from this embryo are used to create replacement organs or tissue, the rest of the embryo will die. But if it grew naturally it would develop into a baby.

Human life begins when an egg cell is fertilised to produce an embryo. Therapeutic cloning would mean that thousands of human embryos would be destroyed after they had been used to donate stem cells.

We do not know how cloning would affect human health. Scientists know that when they attempt reproductive cloning, many embryos die or are disabled. Dolly, the first cloned sheep, is ageing genetically faster than normal. Cloning may result in new disabilities or health problems that we do not know about.

Scientists tried unsuccessfully to clone a healthy sheep 277 times before Dolly was finally born.

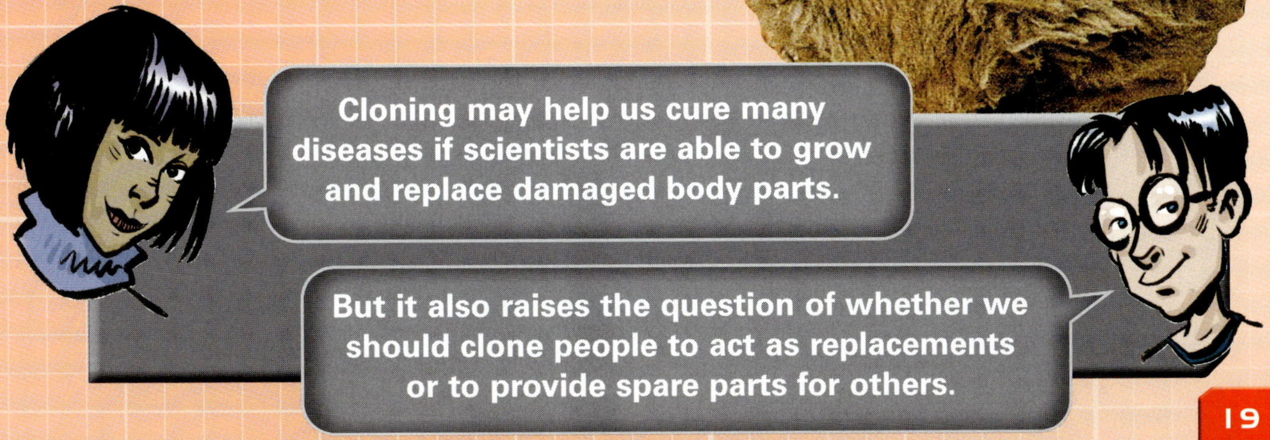

Nuclear power – source of energy or danger?

Science Box

Nuclear power is the name for the energy released by splitting the atoms of the radioactive element uranium. The energy is released as heat which boils water and makes steam to drive electricity turbines.

FOR

Nuclear power already provides seventeen per cent of the world's electricity. It is one of the cleanest and most efficient forms of power. **Nuclear reactors** can be built on small sites. They produce electricity for thousands of people and provide many jobs. The power they can supply is unlimited. There is plenty of uranium left in the Earth's crust and new technology means we will be able to extract sixty times more energy from the uranium than we do today.

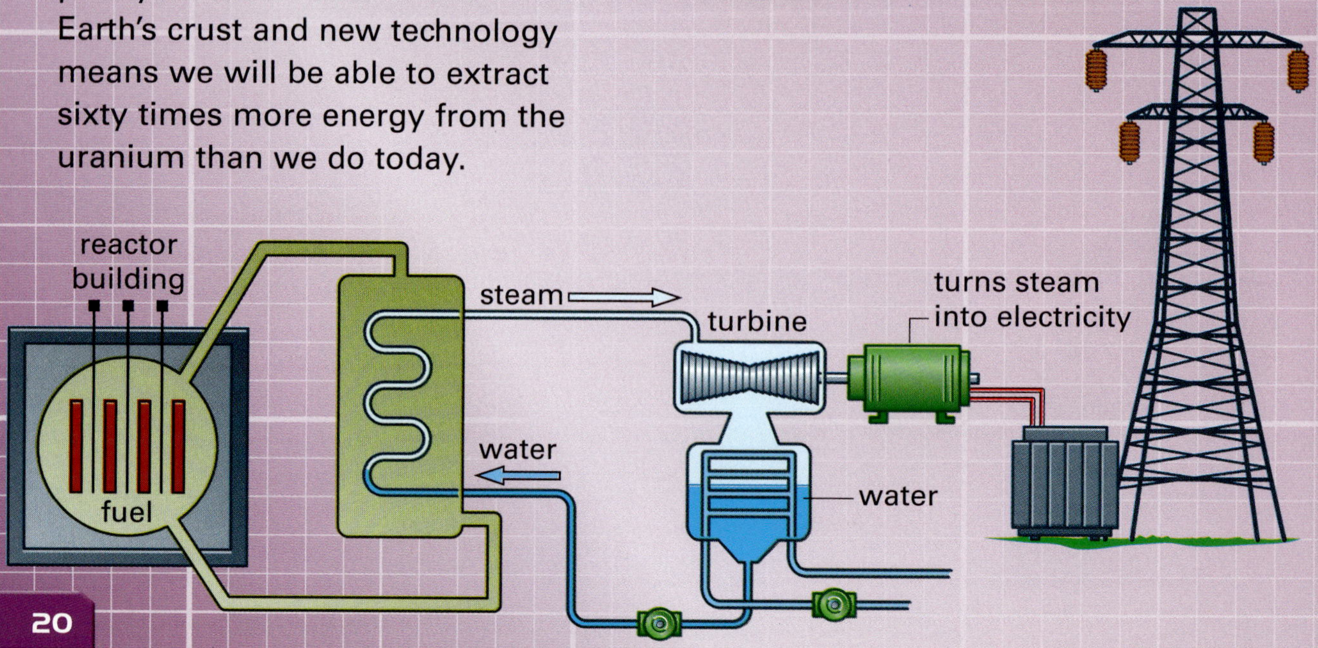

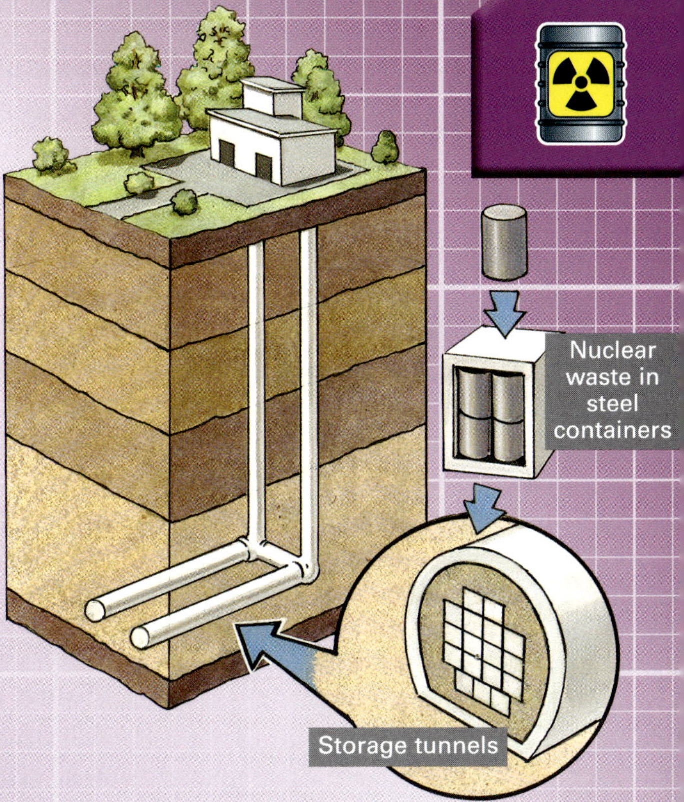

Nuclear power does not cause air pollution or produce greenhouse gases. The radioactive waste produced by reactors can be contained by concrete or steel and cooled down by air or water. Or it can be **reprocessed** to provide fuel for other nuclear reactors.

Nuclear power is getting cheaper as the design of reactors and methods of disposing of waste improve. Nuclear power can help provide the global need for energy in the future, especially in developing countries. Renewable sources of power such as wind and solar power are not available everywhere and cannot meet all our energy needs. Burning fossil fuels such as oil and coal will increase greenhouse gases and global warming.

Containers on their way to a nuclear waste disposal site

AGAINST

Nuclear power is an unsafe technology. High doses of radiation are very dangerous. Nuclear reactors leak some radioactive particles into the environment even when they are operating normally. Scientific studies have shown these leaks can harm the health of people living nearby.

Nuclear power produces hot radioactive waste, which remains dangerous for thousands of years. This waste is a threat to us and future generations. It has to be stored in concrete or steel containers. It takes at least fifty years just to cool down. There is always the risk of storage tanks leaking, or an accident when waste is being transported or reprocessed.

Nuclear power creates plutonium, which is an essential ingredient of nuclear weapons. If more plutonium were made, it might lead to an increase in the numbers of nuclear weapons being made.

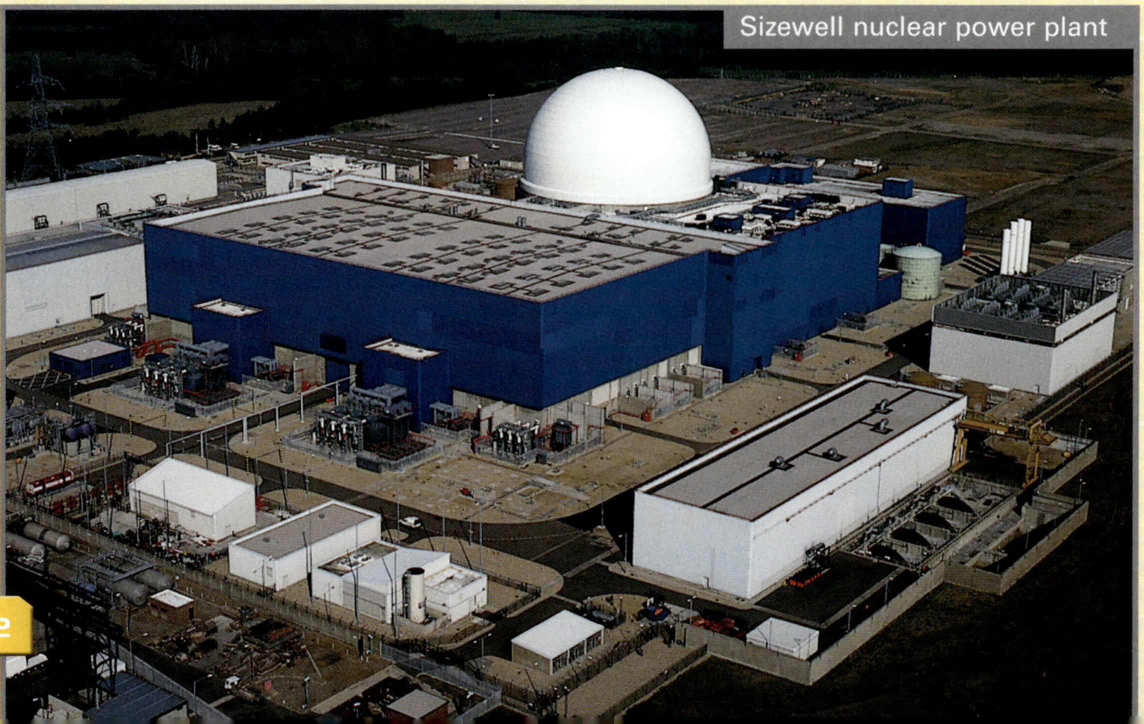

Sizewell nuclear power plant

The damage caused by the nuclear accident at Chernobyl in 1986.

Nuclear reactors are expensive to build because they must have so many safeguards against accidents and leaks. Most reactors are designed to run for around twenty-five years but many are now twenty years older than that. As they age, there is more risk of nuclear leaks and accidents. Major accidents, such as the leak from the Chernobyl reactor in Ukraine in 1986, can release deadly **radioactive fallout** into the environment over thousands of kilometres. This fallout can harm human health, causing cancer and other diseases, and poison the environment for years to come.

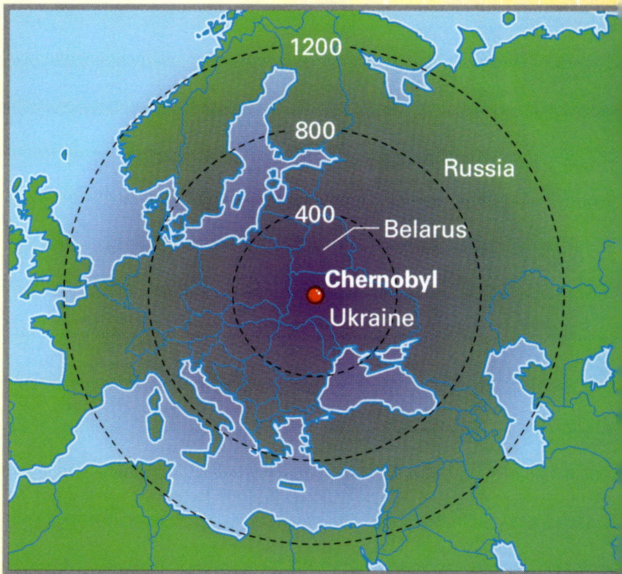

Radioactive fallout was carried many miles from Chernobyl. The worst affected area was Belarus.

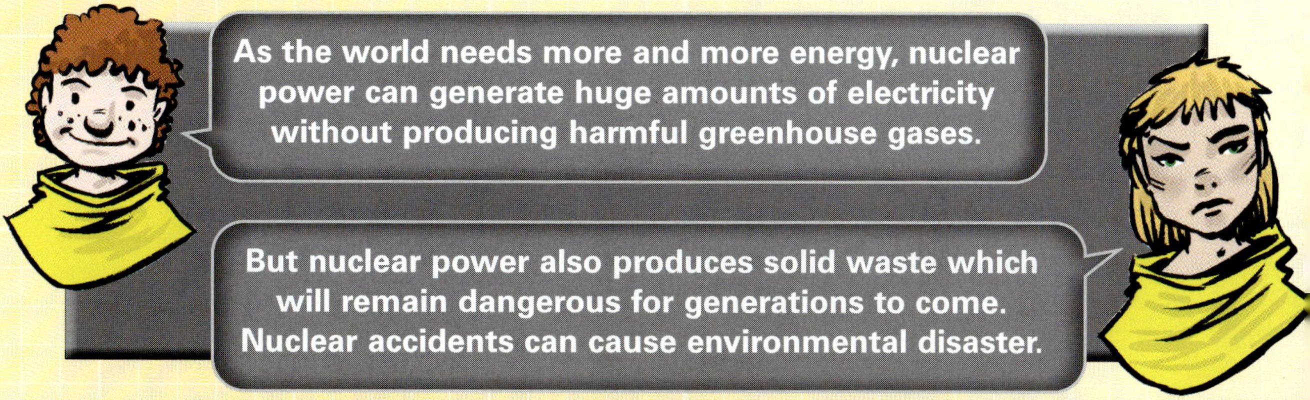

Interactive technology – are we being watched?

Science Box

Scientists can now plant microchips in electronic goods and on our own bodies to create an interactive environment. In future our homes and offices and even our bodies may have computers inside them which can interact with each other.

FOR

Interactive technology can help us in our daily lives. Video recorders can already learn the kinds of television programmes you like and record them for you. When household machines go wrong they will be able to report the fault themselves. So, if your washing machine starts to overheat, it will be able to tell you what is wrong with it.

When you are using computers, you are sending out information as well as receiving it. Sales people can send **cookies** that learn your buying habits. This means that they build up a **database** of the kinds of things you like to buy, so they can offer products and services to suit you. Databases will help us because we will be offered what we want, when we want it.

Interactive technology can also help us feel safe. Mobile phones can have tracking devices built in which means they can locate people to within a few hundred metres. This could help people lost in remote places.

Kevin Warwick, a cybernetics professor, implanted a microchip into his arm that would open doors and turn on lights in his office.

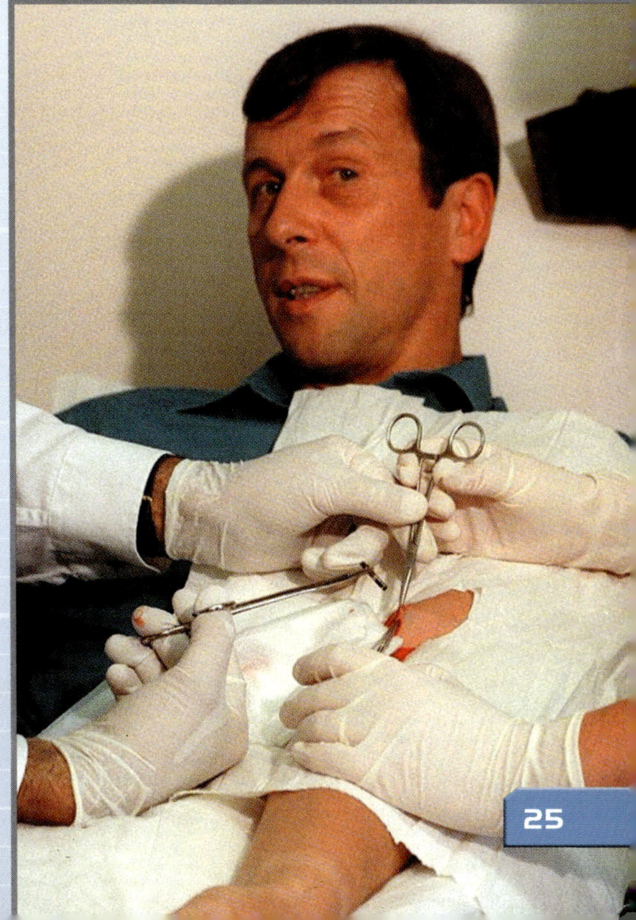

In future, it will be possible to have a tracking device implanted in your body that can exchange signals with microchips in your surroundings. As you come home, the door will open automatically, the lights will switch on, and you will be greeted with a "hello". Interactive technology means we will exchange information with our surroundings to make our lives easier and more comfortable.

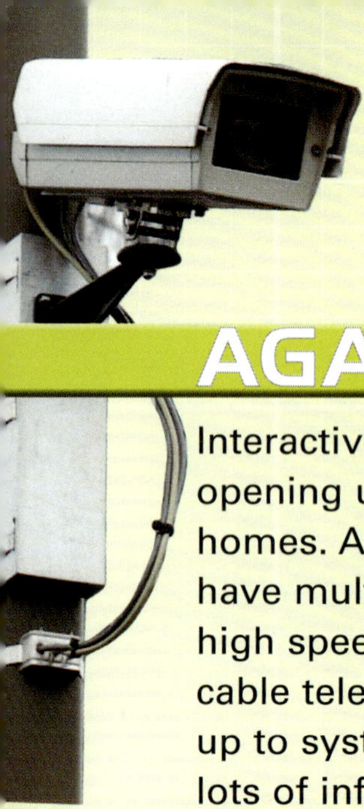

AGAINST

Interactive technology is opening up a spy-hole into our homes. Already many homes have multiple phone lines, high speed Internet links and cable television. We are wired up to systems that are sending lots of information to us but also transmitting other information back from us.

CCTV (closed circuit television) means that we are already being watched in places like supermarkets, offices and car parks. Now people are opening up their homes by being wired up to **webcams** that watch their every move. In future, it may be normal to have our homes monitored by webcams.

FACT: There will be fifty million webcams watching US homes by 2004.

Big companies send cookies to your computer so they can learn what you like to buy. Then the companies bombard you with advertising. This is so they can sell more goods and make more profit.

Every time you use a mobile phone, the network knows where you are. There are tracking devices with location sensing units that can even tell how fast you are moving. They can send the data back via your mobile phone to a computer screen which shows your position on a map.

Companies can learn private information about you from your computer. Then they can buy and sell information about you. For example, an insurance firm could buy the information that you have a gene which could cause illness. The company might refuse to insure you.

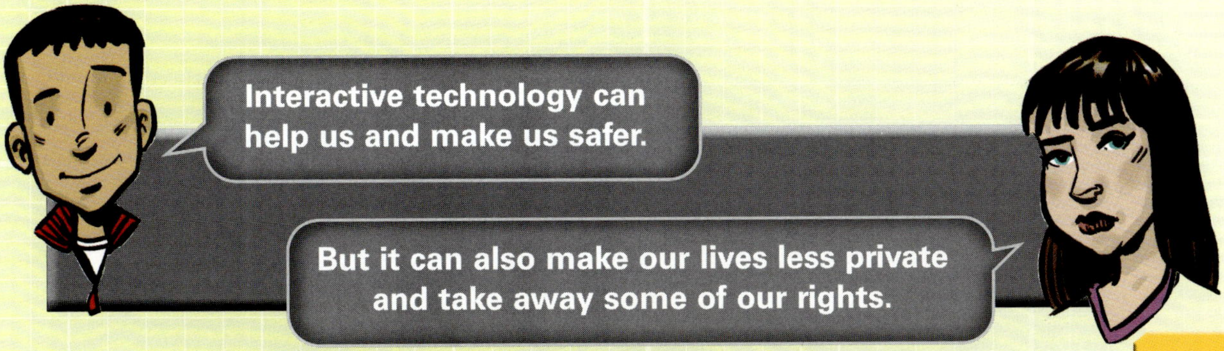

Is it progress?

We all look to scientists to make our lives longer and healthier and to help us understand and care for our world. Everyone hopes for a cure to diseases like cancer. We welcome inventions that help us in our daily lives, like mobile phones or palm top computers.

But sometimes we question new inventions and wonder how they will affect our lives.

We may also be afraid that scientists are going to harm our health. When electric lighting was invented in the 1870s, some people were worried that it was unsafe. In the 1960s, there were health scares about X-rays coming from colour television tubes. Today, there are concerns that mobile phones may release rays which can cause cancer and harm the brain.

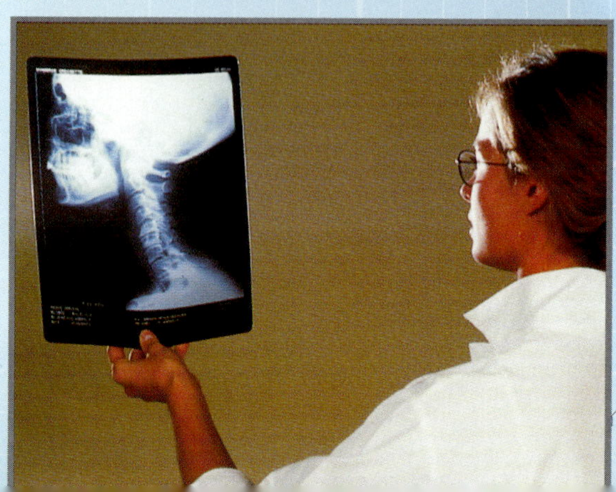

Scientists offer no certainties: except that they will go on making discoveries that have the power to change all our lives. We need to ask whether we want the changes that science offers. We need to think about what is right and what is wrong.

Glossary

acid rain rainfall which has been made into a weak acid due to pollution in the air

allergies when the body reacts badly to something

anaesthetic a drug that causes loss of sensation

antibiotics drugs that cure infections

bio-technology science of producing artificial changes in nature

climate weather systems

computer modelling using computer models to test scientific ideas

cookies a piece of information stored on your computer that tracks all the Internet documents you have viewed

cross-breed produce a new variety from two different types of plant or animal

database computerised file of information

drought a long period without rain

embryo a baby developing in an egg or womb after the egg has been fertilised, or a plant developing from seed

fossil fuels fuels such as oil, coal and gas made from ancient plant remains

genes the units in our body that pass on inherited characteristics

genetics the study of how a parent passes on characteristics through genes

global warming temperature rises caused by the release of greenhouse gases into the Earth's atmosphere

greenhouse gases gases that trap heat from the Sun in the Earth's atmosphere, causing global warming

habitat natural surroundings of an animal or plant

immune system the body's defence system against infection and disease

internal-combustion engine engine in which fuel is burned inside the engine rather than in an outside furnace

microchip a tiny chip of material inside a computer which contains electronic circuits

nuclear reactor site where the chain reaction needed to create nuclear power takes place

nutrition how the body takes in and uses food

organism a living thing such as a plant or animal

radioactive fallout the slow descent of radioactive particles through the atmosphere after a nuclear accident

radioactivity the ability of radioactive materials such as uranium to produce energy when its atoms are split

reprocess recycle nuclear waste

side-effects unwanted reactions in the body to a drug

stem cell special type of cell that can be reprogrammed to become other types of body cell

therapy treatment of disease

transplanted moved into the body from an outside donor

webcam camera linked to a computer to watch the user

Index